HOLY NUDGES

HOLY NUDGES

Marguerite Reiss

Logos International
Plainfield, New Jersey

For Dr. Hugh Missildine, Dr. John Yungblut, Dr. Eugene Mendenhall Jr., and Billie and Jared Darlington, all of whom believed.

Chapters

To find Christ is one thing.

To find Him after a humiliating record of psychiatrists, loss of jobs, attempted suicide, broken marriage and poverty, is quite another.

This is the path the author traveled.

That there must be ways of leading a less troubled, more intelligent life, in spite of an abrasive childhood with parents exhaustingly unsuited to each other, goes without saying. There must be ways of living with dignity and grace and sensible decisions in spite of unacceptable beginnings. There must be ways of integrating the unacceptable beginnings. There must be ways of integrating the unacceptable parts. There must be ways of reaching and finding Him who can integrate that which we cannot.

The dual role of finding and learning to live with one's self and finding and learning to live with Christ is the double-pronged challenge for Christians. It may mean lengthy efforts at psychoanalysis and self-forgiveness. It may mean circumstances of humbling, altar calls, prayer groups. It may mean endless self-analysis, poverty, divorce.

I do not believe "happiness" can be the goal of our lives. But a well-lived life in spite of—and in consideration of— unalterable, inconvenient circumstances, certainly can be. It is this kind of life Christ calls us to and stands ready to help us achieve.

Genesis 28:12
And he dreamed that there was a ladder set up
on earth and the top of it reached to heaven . . .

Revelation 3:8
I know your works. Behold, I have set before
you an open door . . .

There is the door and there is the ladder.
I don't know which is more important.
Both are necessary—
going up
and going in.

I

Who controls you?— directions to open door

You can have books in packages
  houses in packages
    socks, steaks, fruit, popcorn
      fireworks, pencils, thoughts.

Forgiveness may not be necessary but neither is hostility.
You might as well make the choice or someone will make it
for you.

Control by others can look like love, caring, peace.

There is always a yielding of some kind.
But who are we yielding to?

I was fired. I let it happen.
It was a psychological need to be hurt again.
God permitted it. Getting fired was like getting beaten.
Familiar hurt. Similar pain. Control from the past.

It is not the good of life that you are giving yourself that needs to concern you, but what's in control. Let me explain. I knew a man who got more and more money, went more and more places, bought more and more things. He went so many places and bought so many things he neither liked or found use for, that all of the pain was removed. And the aches.
And the longings.
And desires.
And the dimensions he never had, which longings and desire—but not acquisition—could bring.

Am I using my dead parents for an excuse for not writing a book? My psychologist said: "How does it feel to be controlled by the dead?" It felt like a no-answer. Then the situation started changing. My psychologist said: "What I am hearing is that your parents didn't like you—thought you couldn't write. The more you hold yourself to their fantasy, the farther you are from your aim—the book."
What resulted was this: their fantasy got *unaccepted* by me. And I went to the typewriter.

2

It is what you let go of that counts.

I was so frustrated I stopped for cigarettes—the habit I had surrendered to Christ years before. The very first restaurant was empty so I drove on. Traffic lights were against me, parking spots filled; soon, I would be on the freeway and no place for miles. Finally I stopped the car, went in and waited at a gas station for change. I stepped anxiously to the cash register for someone to arrive when I saw "it" taped to the top. It was the unbelievable—a copy of the W. E. Sallman painting of the head of Christ. I turned and fled out of the gas station and drove away.

Thou shalt have no other gods—not even old ghosts. Moving back to the old college town, I saw ghosts of the person I'd wanted to become and hadn't. I never know what to do with ghosts but run. One day I was sent on a story with a photographer accompanying a woman postal carrier who delivered mail in our capital city of 500,000. The woman chose the exact street I had lived on as a student and her first letters were to the rooming house where I lived when I was a sophomore. (A past I still idolized.) It was as though God were saying "Confront your ghosts. Deal with them. Go to the point that stopped you. Then the point beyond."

Into whose hands have you placed the reins of your life?

A need exists to forgive some people quickly. Others to reforgive. With some I cannot. They don't deserve it. This makes me phony and then I have to work harder to forgive myself. (It's either that or be controlled by my phoniness.)

My friend loved me but pushed me back when I got too close. Mostly he had to control. Anyone loving him threatened his control. Then he had to hurt and hurt hard. I got bored with this recurring psychological spin-around . . . love-push away; invite-push back. I walked out.

My life has been a life of the
strongest, most subtle,
most devious dilution.
All the right things
went into it. Diluted.

II

Emphasis—
directions to open door

Where are you putting the emphasis—on believing or not
believing?

Freedom or Slavery?
   Outside of my own case, there are others who hesitate to
be set free for freedom's sake. For a long time I wanted to be
set free so I could select the kind of slavery I preferred to
crawl back into.

Willingness or Faith?
   Again and again it comes back to me: "You don't need
faith as much as a willingness to get into a position of
belief . . ."

What's Going On Inside or What's Going On Outside?
   Today is inner interrogation: As if God might be saying
"Let's move slowly until we find out how you really feel
about what you are trying to do."

   There is movement in the interior of your life. You may
not like it. But you owe yourself the chance to know what it
is; to feel it.

Life is levels of awareness. Life is also levels of emphasis:
Don't forget the past. Put it in a box under the bed and set the alarm clock. When I was married at twenty-six, my husband bought a recipe box for worries. We filed them alphabetically on cards and designated a section of every week categorically to worry. As a result, he never worried. It didn't work for me either. I got the giggles.

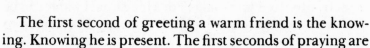

Explore dreams. Dig them out of mothballs. Try them. Maybe they're last year's styles. "You thought it was a security point. It was only a resting point."

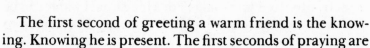

The first second of greeting a warm friend is the knowing. Knowing he is present. The first seconds of praying are not too different.

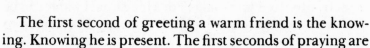

So freedom has cumulative meaning. So it has meaning in immediacy.
So it carries obligation.
But where is the emphasis this time—freedom short-term; freedom long-term; freedom's obligation?

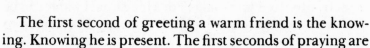

"God change the timing of my hate," is better than "God don't ever let me hate." That emotion (hate) isn't always for all reasons—bad.

There are days when I don't want a coincidence-of-wills. I want God's will pure and simple and I want Him to prod, nudge, explain, follow me into obedience. It's so much easier that way, God. You just tell me and I'll do it.

~~~

(Nor did He have any intention of healing all the sick; radiating blanket-healing wherever He went. I have enjoyed reading that He asked others to take a measure of responsibility for their healing; still others to intervene. He seemed to be after involvement; not hand-outs.)

~~~

Let's talk of combinings. Very often you only have to walk ahead in trust and the very movement blends the colors of your combinings like a watery paintbrush fluidizes blues and reds that coagulated at that last intersection. So live in movement. Walk, dance, *lightly* within your intersections, fluid—like a watery paintbrush and allow, permit, embrace your combinings. It is not necessary to nail down your combinings, experiences, relationships; tag, label, categorize and file. Dip the paintbrush into the water and let it mix the colors. Watch them. Combine. Flow!

~~~

Dr. Elton Trueblood said all life may be worth one weekend. For that matter all of one life may be worth one good deed, one sacrificial act, one printed article, one inspiration. All of the strands of all of the threadings in the tapestry of each of our lives do not have to weave patterns. Some can hang out and make fringe.

Jesus wasn't minimizing power. He healed the blind man. But it took a combination. *Your* faith (in yourself); *your* wanting (to be healed); *my* channels to the Father. *Our* interacting. All of that. Healing came last. First came his question to the blind man: "What do you want me to do for you?" Awareness!

Unfulfillments? Take these before Christ. Not for magic. For dialogue.

Almost from the beginning when I went into Christ-centering, I was running into people who demonstrated coldness, almost hate. Then one day I woke up to the fact God was revealing weaknesses in them I hadn't been able to see. One newspaper executive had been unkind. When we talked one day he lost his spectacles and bending over after them, his stomach became a rolling ball sagging up under the inside of his shirt. It looked grotesque, almost clown-like.

My ex-husband ranted at me, but all the time I was noticing his tiny feet in brown suede shoes like he had been a child I had known many, many years ago.

Balance is so important. Pain unbalanced by good leads to too much pain. Too much suffering leads into stultification. When fatigue overtakes, it may be one droplet of balancing God has wedged into our lives. His method of saying "slow down."

The looms of our lives need not be tangled just because a few threads hang out. Every thread doesn't always have to be completely blueprinted into the full design. Maybe the design wants to change. Some designs have distinct parts. When I yielded to this whole idea, I noticed every pinprick of every design in the art gallery wasn't perfect. It's the dominance of the design that corrects my perspective; and advances it. This is true of art and of life.

It is the flavor, color, scent of the encounter with you that is important—not all things being perfect. When I am with you, I feel good, but that "good" depends on a lot of other balancings. I should not want every minute beside you. All minutes are not always good, always at your side. I must stand alone. Walk alone. And if you are in my life that makes an extra special flavor, color, scent, dominance.

III

Yielding—rung one

"Yield the discomfort as a sacrifice."
"But I can't get rid of it that way."
"*You* are not supposed to get rid of it."
"Then why yield the discomfort?"
"That you may be given the gift of removal."
"And, if I am not?"
"God will place it in perspective."

～～

Whenever I deal from fear, He backs off. Like He doesn't want to help me perpetuate my fear even if it means He has to wait. My husband beat with hands and words and I finally got around to praying I might help him. But I wanted to help him because I was afraid because of his tendencies to violence, not because I wanted Christ in my life or loved my husband. I was dealing from fear. Cold fear. And for nineteen years nothing happened.

11

It is when we fail to call pain *pain* that healing is delayed. Neither loss should ever be called gain. It may be incorporated into a larger whole and renamed in its greater context. But on its smaller existent level, loss is still loss. I spent nineteen years in a survival marriage. I ceased to grow. Every day I told myself I was happy. Those 19 years were a valley I trudged through to reach a mountain where the air is peaceful and clear. But the years I lost were nineteen lost years.

———

I'm learning. I had been enjoying the familiarity of what happened in my childhood happening in my adulthood. The hammer-hammer of my father saying "There's something wrong with you" became the hammer-hammer of my husband saying "Who would ever hire you?" I felt good about pain. It was familiar.

Then something inside started wanting to push me out of sickness. Somebody prayed for me. A thousand times I dreamed, tried, stumbled. I lost a lot of jobs, a house, a marriage, $7,000. What was the answer? Give in to Christ, for in retaining horror—even a portion of past horror—you are precluding life. Forgiveness was not a question. Yielding was. For in yielding you are yielded to—and the hammering stops.

———

Don't identify the box as you, the job as you, the problem as you, the labels as you, the hungers as you.

IV

Miracles take us up and in

A miracle always arrives at the impact of tragedy. The tragedy could have gone farther. Restraint is the miracle. Some days the most any of us are able to say is "Thank God it is no worse."

⁓

Basic to levels of healing are levels of willingness.

The 5,000 became willing to be made a fool of, to see a mad man take a basket to feed a crowd. To stretch . . . elasticize . . . change the selves they had brought along to the selves He made them see (vessels through which a miracle was being produced).

Wasn't Jesus healing people when He asked their humility, risk, willingness to be made a fool of, belief they'd seen a miracle, deeper belief they'd been a part of one?

Wasn't filling stomachs secondary?

⁓

The loaves and fishes was a second-hand miracle.

The real miracle with the 5,000 was what happened inside them before they ate a crumb.

Scorn. Disbelief. Shock. Willingness to believe. To accept the unbelievable. To see themselves as a miracle worthy of being saved, worthy of being fed.

Maybe the most significant part of the miracle is the image-stretching down inside the miraclized person. It is one thing to watch a miracle. Another thing to be a part of one.

━━≫⊱

Timing to a miracle? Staggered timing to a miracle? All those people didn't get their nourishment at the same, precise, pin-second. Somebody got his first. But I don't like somebody getting ahead of me when it's my miracle too. You mean, I have to become humbled and wait and pray and be patient and reach out and forgive even in a miracle, Lord?

━━≫⊱

Give me the guts, Lord, to stay in the nothingness until I've learned its teaching.

━━≫⊱

V

Frames—rung two

The hurt is one thing. The frame you place it in to keep it dustless is quite another.

━━━➤

When I was married and we camped and ran out of coffee cups, using dirty ones over and over was "just outdoor living," my husband said. When we had company for Thanksgiving dinner and a piece of dirt clung to the china, everybody made apologies.

━━━➤

My son got shot but he lived. His ripped-up leg got so healed he won track records. Then a year and a half later I lost custody of him in a hearing I didn't have anything to say about.

    Lost—custody
    Won—leg/life

After I noticed how it was, I knew that God had built my winning into my losing. He works that way.

━━━➤

A friend of mine was so famous he had a million dollar building named after him. But when his only daughter died, he kept a tally of the condolence cards he got. He did not tell me about his grief but about how many personal notes he had received.

Funny, but "bad childhood" becomes at last a picture I keep carrying needing reframing. I feel like taking the picture out of the glass and the frame that says "poor me" and mounting it on silver.

"All of a sudden you realized beatings were schooling. Preparation."

"You were sensitized by your scarring—did you forget?"

I don't know why. But I feel suddenly sad that most of us waste our sensitizings. I think of the times we forget there is something beyond for which we were being readied to carry out instructions.

~~~

Sunday in silent Quaker Meeting a young child cried. The mother did not care. I provided the anger myself. Finally I walked out of the Meeting to meditate. God seemed to get through outside and in three blocks, I had four answers. Why on earth had I wasted that anger over the child crying?

~~~

Can I get to the point of so knowing Christ, that I am grateful His sacrifice was made so that I have the courage I need to make mine?

16

VI

Relationships—rung three

There are levels of relating.

~~~

I got interested in "good" relationships and interested in "bad" relationships. My discovery when I looked at every one I'd ever had was sidetracking. There were good moments in every relationship. And bad moments too. That's what I finally learned.

I got reinterested then in counting good seconds in encountering people I had come to know. That was different entirely from "good people" counting or "bad relationships" tallying.

~~~

You can sell yourself on sex as a creative outlet. But for that matter, there's creative killing.

17

There is a time when the orange peel in the garbage can be sweet. The weekend was beautiful because I accepted the fact that we were camping, not at the Hilton; cooking bacon in slacks and boots, not at the Ritz; looking at iced trees in the park, not the opera in Paris. By accepting and inviting God creatively into my limitations, I found release: the orange peel in the garbage tasting sweet.

There is a stark reality to the cross that has nothing to do with Christmas. The cross on the church outside my window was unadorned, speckled by birds, greying from the weather of many winters.

I noticed the cross because I was noticing the fingermarks of that January day—a courtroom with a woman (me) and a man I had married nineteen years before challenging custody of one of our sons. Legal manipulations. I had worked hard to forgive. Crazy thoughts but I begged God to bring Christ closer, whatever anyone did to me; make me a channel; obliterate my hostility. Something tore at me—rage, maybe. Why had I prayed for the man causing disturbance with my child, bringing us all into court stupidly, five years after divorce?

Sections of me tore off, like an amputated leg. I wanted to win. And win hard . . . and to hate. I wanted to get out of "pray for your enemies,"—"God will bring you through every battle."

I was feeling very God-abandoned, Christ-forsaken, stupid. Suddenly I was thinking about Bonhoeffer, a martyr in Germany. The Infinite selects the one who gets nothing but being chosen. Bonhoeffer was hanged. That had little to do with my fifteen-year-old son in a January courtroom. But it hit me hard.

And that weather-worn, unglittered cross on the church roof next to my kitchen when I got back home wasn't pleasing either.

Today I developed a shred of hostility. It was well deserved. The other person worked hard for it. It was honest (the encounter we had)—honest hate—justifiable hostility. What feels less good is keeping it. I really want to keep it. It is hard to give up what I want to keep.

Christ said "Why has Thou forsaken me?" In great pain, in intense fear, in moments of deep distress, cries to the Lord go unheeded. But there are levels of forsaking! Every relationship has times of forsakenness.

Everyone doesn't have to be an important person in my life. Most become a bit of tinsel, a sticker somewhere on the side that identifies something special about the whole. Some people are directional, like a mailing label on a package. Or a postage stamp—without them things wouldn't have moved through that particular intersection. When I look at people this way, I quit expecting them to be all things for me. But even better, I cease expecting the postage stamp to always remain usable. Most postage stamps get canceled.

19

Respect your life energy. So often the object of your hostility isn't worth one more heartbeat of your livingness. Some moments deserve only your non-response.

All aspects of every situation do not have to be pleasing or nourishing or promising. Some can be utterly grotesque. But it is the focus, the emphasis, the dominance that counts.

Being very vulnerable to limited people is not synonymous with being vulnerable to Christ. The latter could mean walking away from certain people.

Jesus doesn't act like you have something crawling on you. Why should you?

Breaking a Relationship
I have been thinking of two dogs I happened to watch tugging over a rope. I noticed how much difficulty was involved in both dogs letting go immediately. One of the animals had to be first to let go, if by split seconds. So with a relationship. A simultaneous release is impossible. It takes a small letting go to establish a big letting go. Our days are made up of smaller "letting go's." We never arrive at the big letting go in any kind of simultaneity—not the same time, the same day, via the same method.

VII

Somewhere on the ladder

Sugar is a substitute for reality my sister said of her habit of sweets. Food can be compulsion. So can sex, sleep, busyness, money, travel, titles . . . I can give myself all kinds of good things in order to take me from me.

It is a shock to jump when you've never walked;
To walk when you're used to crawling;
To crawl when you're used to lying down.
Remember the man by the pool?
His words to Christ were not
"Oh, Lord put me in the water." But—
"Lord, I cannot."
In that statement lay his stability.

If God would only be my absentee Landlord pointing the way, taking the blame, life would be so much simpler. So much!

Spiritual time doesn't have to be a sandwich devoured within a package of microseconds. Look back over a period of years and add up the "God crumbs." The key word is "Add." A crumb of His guidance yesterday added to a crumb from today builds the bridge you will cross over tomorrow.

VIII

Rickety ladders, shaking ladders

There are times when life begins to go wrong, a venture runs amok; when in the balance of alternatives, it is better not to turn—but to let the wrongdoing run its course—to be grounded. And in being grounded—to learn a good lesson.

~~~

I wanted an apartment when my house was sold and there wasn't one. Then I acted, thanking Jesus for His caring and moved children and furniture into the first one I was able to spot which wasn't Guidance. A year later, after forfeiting the down payment to unscrupulous landlords, we moved away. I said I "had" to move into; and "had" to move out of. And that God—both times—answered my prayer. He did. He answered my prayers with choices. Not commands. I didn't "have" to move either which-way. I chose to. What happened was my hurry-up-ness. I could have waited, looked longer, searched farther, knocked harder. What I learned about that debacle was (1) don't blame God for wrong moves (2) don't lunge into self-hate over a wrong apartment.

Miserable in life, they lie there in such an incredible lie: "Together Forever." I only whispered at the restaurant maid when I needed to scream and my sister and aunt chatted about "the lovely grave we saw over there at the cemetery." Suddenly I was alone again, crawling in a dungeon of childish horror when one parent screamed at the other who beat me and screamed once again. And yet was it not I who was entombed? The recording machine played monotonously in the restaurant and people chatted over jello and soup; and the cemetery flowers stood forthright and the bronzed plaques rested and shone in the dazzling sunlight. And the cemetery was as we had left it. And the restaurant was as we had found it. And I "lay" in my "casket" of the stark, sheer horror of the remembrance of the dungeon of my childhood, and nobody would let me out. I had to find my own way out

IX

Nudges, leadings, guidance

To be led by God doesn't mean to be conducted through.
A leading isn't a rail pass.
It is a direction signal.

Guidance must entail levels of awareness, quietness, listening-ness, realizations we don't get answers in one minute—even one week. They come in crumbs, whisps, shadings, shadows, specks, filterings—in converging lines of evidence.

(Why does God teaspoon guidance when He could atom bomb it?)

Sometimes it's like He places a gentle hand on my shoulder and holds me back (a restraining).

25

A built-in restraining? There is also the built-in miracle. I parked by the library and a car came along and took my door, scattering broken glass over my arms and chest and onto the road. *Restraining!* The glass chunks hit no child. *Miracle!* Another car drove up. They had seen the accident, gone home, prayed about it, returned to stand by and become friends.

————

Guidance means picking up crumbs out of the market place.
  Things people say that stand out.
    Light bulb remarks.
      Synchronicity of small events.
        Coincidences.
          Above all read street signs!

————

I got a holy nudging to do a story on Arch Willard of "The Spirit of 1776." Driving home from a shopping center, I saw a toy called "Spirit of 1776." And two street signs simultaneously, "Willard Street" and "Hope Street." I went in the house and got my notes.

————

Tonight, I asked God how we could have been lucky enough that the president of a large university intervened and saved my son's scholarship at a small Ohio college. Then, I looked up from the steering wheel. The intersection I just went through was "Grace Street."

Coincidences, Hold Times, Knowings

Communicating with God is very often like breaking through walls of granite only instead of cutting tools, one works with silence, levels of listenings, strange happenings, coincidences.

━━━➤

My story came back. I prayed for a market and leafing through a writer's magazine I spotted a former editor's name who meant a great deal. I glanced across that same page for "guided" addresses, found one, wrote to them, the story came back and a year later, I still hadn't revamped the piece. What had happened? Now I know. In the long span of guidance, much can be said to be coincidence and only that.

━━━➤

I met a man, fell in love and couldn't forget him. Then two days later there was a "knowing" that told me "no" as definite as a scent in a room, a flavor in a pudding, the breeze that I feel blowing my hair at night. I could not see, capture, catch or define such a "knowing." And it had no voice, color, substance. It stole over me like cold, covered me like light. It was logical and intelligent. It contained a truth I did not want. But, like night, I could not wipe it away. I had to live with it. And still do.

27

"If it's God's will, it will happen" my friend said.
"But, I want to *make* it happen," I said.
"Then you can't tell whose will it is," my friend replied.

I wanted to go to Vancouver to live with my friend but for a long time nothing broke open. God knew I was willing to wait if He would be sure to spring the miracle. I reviewed my case with Him every year. No nudging. As though He was still stopping me, not letting me. Then, as though He wasn't saying "Go" or "Stop" either. Not saying anything. Which was His way of saying something. I had to take the trip to figure out what He had in mind.

Some nudgings are "wait a minute" signs. These are different from underlinings.

But this is how the process of guidance reaches most of us—pretty blurry, nevertheless real. Our job is to work something through blurriness into focus.

Mistaken guidance will be (can be) woven in, not just washed aside. There's a difference.

I was reading my journal from five years and I realized so much of what I thought was guidance was not. My son misread words when he was in first grade. Other grades too. But in each instance, he was learning to recognize. Now he reads very well. So, with guidance.

―――

There is explicit guidance and implicit guidance. You discover something when you put this to work.

―――

It was a week of living in fear. I was afraid I would not get a job. I was to meet a friend for an interview but slow traffic brought me almost to a stop. Clocking my losing time, I almost gave up. Yet, I realized I would have to keep driving. I prayed, "Dear Lord, lead me from this wrong way to the right road and cause them to wait for me." Oddly the strange highway emptied into an unusual circular drive some miles beyond and I arrived at the plant at exactly the right time we had decided upon. Sometimes I do not understand God's timing and I cannot see my destination. I feel utterly hopeless, terrifyingly lost but God has knowledge of circular drives I don't have.

―――

All nudgings are not leadings. Often the Holy Spirit seems content to simply say our thoughts are mingling.

We are led by threads; baited by little beginnings of guidance that fade out of our lives, but come back with glow-power later on, like a color that disappears in a tapestry to appear with surprise in the border. Like the old-fashioned previews of coming attractions that took up theatre time in the 1930s.

Look not for answers, but for crumbs. Threads of conversation that are "Lord-flavored." Coincidences, underlinings, bits of words and phrases tacked into dialogue. Read street signs. Think of Him putting His arm around your shoulder and saying "I know. I know. I am waiting with you. We are together in the waiting. We'll move at the right time."

God gives drawstrings of certainties.

I draw them across miles and years, over gravestones, and heads and shoes and miles. Driblets of messages from dropped words, spoken words, shouted words. Experiences which tied together spell out a deepening, a shading, a silhouetting—God's voice getting to me louder. It's good to keep notes on your nudgings.

The Too-Much Prayer

Perhaps He is saying if you pray for a billion universes to be constructed overnight, this will not occur. It is the too-

30

much prayer. But if you ask His will—lagging just a feather behind to allow and make sure of Christ's position of leading and yours of following, you'll be led to know something about your piece of the action at a certain time.

X

Without honesty
the ladder falls, the door bolts

We call war, protection. We call survival-marriage, happy couplehood. When my friend was eighty years old, we called him eighty years "young." My mother said we had a happy childhood. She said "Your father pays his bills. Don't shake your dirty linen before the neighbors."

If I am living in Hell I want to know I am living in Hell, for from that beginning I can work my way out.

~~~

No matter how bad my dilemma, no matter how unsolvable, no matter how unspeakable among Christians, the rocky edges of my life are where I meet Him—not in church, at the altar, at the communion rail, early Sundays. No matter how staggering the precipice on which I walk, I can refuse to invite Him into it. Or, I can invite Him in.

He waits to point me to a higher level and to straighten out the level on which I am existing.

(He can enter into my love affairs and ease my rejection . . . the pressures of singleness.)

In His greatness He removes my need to hate. I can show Him the civil war within where my outer self wants to thrive and my inner soul begs to fail.

I prayed for someone to love me which was phony because what I wanted was the awareness that someone loved me. A difference. I fished around until I found within myself a whole set of fears that people might not love me. I needed to be released from that more than I needed a human being who would favorably react to me. I had this sore need for reaffirmation, confirmation, repetitious approval many years before I recognized it.

A real loss is a real loss and must be faced exactly that way. One day I purchased a series of opera tickets. They were choice seats for performances in a city 250 miles away. When the opera week approached, it became obvious that I could not attend and could not sell the tickets. I was doubly miserable. I spent several days commiserating until a friend pointed out "You *made* a mistake; you are not a mistake. Keep the distinction clear." Still, I had to face squarely that I paid fifty dollars for tickets I didn't use.

Guidance to what? To another level of guidance? To Holy obedience? To another person? I left my job and God found me another paying twice as much. Was it guidance? Some of it was. A lot of it was stumbling.

Disappointment is still disappointment though it may be served on a platter of joy.

I don't always wish to not fail. I don't like this about myself. There is stability to the continuity even of failing. There is such a thing as a security blanket of fears; a satin comforter of rejection. Decorative failure.

———

Real loss faced—real imbalances shouldered—real pain suffered leads through sadness, agony, on to healing. It is when we fail to call pain *pain;* and loss *loss;* and tragedy *tragedy* that healings are delayed. Loss should never be called less than loss; or emptiness less than emptiness. It may be incorporated into a larger whole, into an expanded insight, and renamed; but on its smaller existent level, it is still a pain or a loss or an emptiness or an aloneness. All of that.

———

Distinguish between desire and expectation—sexual desire, sexual expectation; job desire, job expectation; writing desire, writing expectation. Get under the crust so you can clarify which you are to deal with.

———

I have to come to a point where my self-acceptance is strong enough to permit me to forgive myself for my un-growth. It took fifty years.

Not everything has to be yielded. Not infrequently my desire is to yield that which, inside me, says "No—get busy and do something about this yourself."

Sometimes when I go to my typewriter with great anticipation, nothing happens. Then I have to yield the anxiety that nothing will happen again and again. Sorting this out, putting my faith in myself and God as well as the typewriter moves things along.

<hr />

Not: what is happening between us? But: what is going on inside while the happening is between us? Do I bathe myself in warm responses? Is warmth between us—a happening?

<hr />

The simple facing of winter is possible only if you *feel* cold and *see* snow and *note* barren-ness. Winter is not summer. Winter is winter; shock is shock; aloneness, aloneness; fear, fear. But know above all there is He who leads, who loves, who waits, wholly dependable—on whose shoulders you can lean, with whose understanding you can commit your life whether you are given the package of relief you desire in the quantity in which it is preferred, or not.

<hr />

5:30 a.m.

Was the experience so awful had it been shared? Suddenly I thought of death. I thought of it because I had just noticed I hadn't heard the drum of traffic on the street. Or breathing in the next room either. And I lay there sliding away from first awareness that it was a holiday without my son in his room, or the town. All that remained was the feeling of too much peace. Like something that could go on forever, an eerie thing, a Hell of no voices, no disturbance, no pain, no problem, no task, no worry—only peace. Separation. It was like a joke. A foreverness in the Hell of total aloneness. I wanted someone to talk to, to share it. I thought of someone to share it. There was no one. Only Peace—to which I addressed the inevitable question: "Is this like death?"

XI

Levels of happiness— the goal is the search

There are levels of happiness. But by clinging to one we make the others impossible.

Resaid: Our experience in happiness is in levels. By not clinging to one vision, we make the other possible.

━━≈⠃⠇

Life is *not* fair. There are many who give ten percent for a ninety percent yield. I knew a man who lied, manipulated, amassed a fortune, retired as president of a junior college, had prominence, influence, a healthy family, was integrated and motivated. True, he lived the life of the encased. He never found out the person he could have become. But his fictitious self is happy. I cannot say he is not. I do say there are levels of happiness.

━━≈⠃⠇

The search when it is lost is such a loss.
The search for wholeness.

I am free to overflow but not to demand a reward for my overflowing.

The searching is the reward, the knowing that crumbs and flakes of guidance can be trusted; that God cares and Christ holds the blueprint; that you are going toward it and wholly right in your search.

Cell multiplication is a miracle. Within miracles lie boundaries. So God wills it. Boundaries! Things need limits—even miracles—even cell multiplication. We forget to thank God for the limits around things but they are markedly important. I wouldn't want unleashed cell multiplication. That's cancer. Or everyone to love me in all ways at all times. Too much love-miracle. I couldn't handle it. Or to have all the money I'd like. Or to live forever. When I think about limits, there's a lot of my life that I need to probe through that I call unhappiness which isn't.

XII

Listening—rung four

It is the thrust of agony that causes us to reach
  To beg
    To cry
      To wait
        To yield
          To begin again—hushed,
            To listen.

———

There are times when it seems all Christ is saying through my confusion is "Let's clarify."

———

I walked on the high mountain when I had been divorced nearly a year. Looking over the valley was like looking across a life of fears—fears my parents "gave" me, fears I took, mostly the fear of myself. When my husband spoke, I listened and when he said something was wrong with me, I listened to that, too. I let people tell me what was "good" in terms of babies, houses, Boy Scouts, home baked bread, my feelings. And for a long time I tried to sit on my feelings, the ones people said weren't good and I shouldn't keep.

41

Sometimes He isn't saying "Go here," but rather, "How do you feel about this situation?"

—⤳—

I was wrestling with inner growth only I didn't know it. I thought I was just unhappily married. I came up out of the basement carrying wash and a verse struck my eyes from a wall calendar. "Behold, I have set before you an open door . . ." Shortly after that a school superintendent offered me my first big job. That bought a psychiatrist's help and two years later, a divorce. After that I traveled the country and began to write. It had indeed been an open door.

—⤳—

I got mad and carried on but my sister was exceptionally calm. She answered my apology by saying "It was your struggle. I remained firm. You were fighting yourself against me and I stood still while it was going on."

—⤳—

Christ communicating some new direction to us—must be like melting the Rock of Gibraltar. Is it any wonder He takes us by the hands, the ears, the feet, hunger points, disaster pangs? He competes with TV, outer space, planned packaging, computerization. Maybe He becomes grateful when we grasp faith even if we don't hang on.

(I think He lets me yank Him. But it makes me weak and tired to think I've been yanking at Jesus all day.)

Beneath the sexed-up man is the hurt boy who wanted to throw his truck. I occasionally got in the way and the sexed-up man said he loved me but he wanted to throw his truck. And he threw it. And I got in the way again. It took me a long time to figure all this out.

XIII

Easy climbing

"Here I am Lord, send me, but not until after the car gets fixed."

———

Easings In

I find that Christ provides the flavoring sometimes as salt in the food. His unseen influence provides an "easing"— something new, scant redirection, re-flavor, newness of taste. Without the grains of seasoning the stew is almost unpalatable. Once there is salt, that portion of life becomes suddenly remarkably different. One morning, dark, on a bus going to work, I didn't have ten cents with me for a morning paper describing my friend's death. A poor woman in an old coat was reading and I asked her if I could see the obituary after she finished. "Please take the paper because I've read it and I'm through." Her gesture eased in Christ. I thought of Him. It helped my grief.

45

Light Nudgings
   A friendship had broken. I blamed myself and brooded. Suddenly I looked up from notes lying dormant by my typewriter to books on the shelf, one of which yielded its title along the spine. Unbelievingly I read: "The Lost Half Hour." It had been thirty minutes since the self-belittling began. Was it a nudging—God saying "Okay. Now let's get back to work"?

        —◅◅

   Humble asking is the beginning of a power-tap. We must literally speak out our askings. Over and over again and again.

        —◅◅

   I traveled one Sunday to a town where my sister lived in a mansion tucked in winding hills. I prayed "Lord lead me without backtracking. Even as you lead me now through life." I suffered doubts. Finally, her house stood among the trees. I got there along the shortest route—by prayer, but also with all my antennas up, feeling my way.

        —◅◅

(Why didn't Christ sequin-up a miracle?
   Fish aren't glamorous.
      Or loaves of bread.
         Shifting about a mountain
            or two would have been much
               more impressive, Lord.)

Sometimes it seems God leads me even to sales. I found valances reduced to twenty-five cents. I didn't have much money. They looked bright and cheery. Sometimes it takes the tangible—like curtains—to bring God into my mind.

———

Sometimes I know my friends by their fears.

———

Suddenly it occurred . . . spiraling circles of prayer unfoldment. I closed my eyes at my desk picturing prayer loops circling from the blotter to the floor and down the hall and up under the boss's door and around them both. After the first few minutes it was easy. I could easily continue picturing these twirling prayer-loops entwining the two I prayed for—the boss and my friend; and, coiling, around them securely. The next day my friend stopped by to report the whole interview with her boss a big success. Did the prayer loops help? Yes!

———

Be glad you learn spiritually—*slowly*. A tooth yanked out without sedative leaves the patient missing more than a tooth.

———

I had physical unanswereds and I couldn't do anything about them. I started for the health spa but it was too cold and I walked around the apartment, tried to sleep, listened to the undercurrent of the children's TV sets upstairs while holding within my attention the personality of Christ in my living room. Finally it came from me "Okay, Lord, we'll go." Fifteen minutes later I was exercising and advancing into steam and hot baths and feeling the return of health and balance. Big decisions are not always asked of me.

～～

My son and I talked from Alaska over an electrical conduit for an intense few minutes letting an eccentric piece of power-filled "string" do the work. I can't explain how the "work" is done. I realize the telephone wires work. My son is a continent away. But crazily we are in immediate contact. I know it—he knows it—and the knowing of it becomes all-important. The fine points of how many miles of cable over which mountains is not my point of focus. We are in contact. Prayer is like that. Contact.

～～

One day I got in a gigantic transcontinental plane bound for England. The plane's crew were bustling through the aisles, stewardesses handing out pillows, stewards answering questions about the flight. It had taken me weeks to get ready and all of my life to dream about the trip. I could see the pilot and co-pilot seated in front of a complex instrument panel checking out first one set of gauges and then another. Luggage finally was put on board and the luggage doors locked. The engines were started, checked, kept going. Clearance was given and the great jet rolled slowly down the runway—a voyage over 2,000 miles of water.

Since that time, I have flown many times but I never take

off without amazement at the amount of preparation that goes on before a flight. I noted a similar amount of preparation when I was wheeled into the operating room. All of the technicians, the nurses, the discussions, instruments, cleanliness seemed to indicate great preparedness.

There is an analogy between flying and "taking off with the Lord." He has assured us He is there when we pray. Each situation on my knees is different, but some require real sweating work before I'm off the ground and He's co-piloting.

XIV

A worthy goal is not a "should

A worthy goal is not a should. A worthy goal is a worthy goal.

~~~

I go to Kenyon College to visit my son. I am bored with his world. My "should self" says "You should love him." Then, I know that a brief touching down is all that is needed. I do not need to enter his world but to walk through it on my way back into mine.

~~~

Let the imbalance be, until a new balance moves in.

~~~

Mis-action often requires a working through rather than an apology. Never say I'm sorry when you are in reality apologizing to yourself for being strong enough to work something through. A working-through may be strange, or not strange. But a working-through is sometimes necessary and should not be apologized for.

Unearned guilt is yours to keep, not give away even if it is your leverage into another's sympathies.

─────

Begin with your separateness, your imbalances, your aloneness, your disconnectedness, and invite Him in. Christ deals with all these things.

─────

Justifiable jealousy exists but look in back of it. I was living in an apartment with my son for fifty dollars a month happily writing and I was jealous of my sister's $60,000 home where her kids wrecked their cars and someone always came up with a new one. None of this was important—except what I *wasn't* facing.

─────

In five years of divorce I never conquered certain forms of unfulfillment. I never did have the courage to ask help via a prayer group. The cost of admitting was too great. If I'd asked them to pray for me they might have lectured. I wasn't willing to take the risk. So, I over-ate and we all prayed about that.

─────

"When you really want to save the Temple—when you are really living for Me—for Me in you—then you'll live differently. Not self-sacrifice. Not anticipation. But, love for Me. Then you'll build on the life within. Then you'll put aside the worries about the sparrows and the bread and the man to love."

XV

Baggage up ladder, through door

Baggage
You reached your alonenesses by yourself. Alone you must learn the lessons of its deeper dimensions. How? —hourly yielding, "having" faith, that He who knew the most prolonged aloneness will bring you out. And He will. But only, I think, when He has allotted us sufficient time for learning to have taken place. For it is indeed our growth He is for, not our suffering, though the one sometimes drags along the other.

Grow away from the syndrome of starting the day accepting unearned guilt and then self-punishing for guilt you didn't earn.

The fishermen dropped their nets and *then,* empty-handed, followed.

XVI

Confront ladder—confront door

Confront

The Instant Attack
The way is to instantly blast off, not peek around the rear pew of our lives . . . for a glimpse. Confront Him. Today, now. He said, seek, ask, knock. I dug out a place under my high, old-fashioned bed to go seek His presence when nothing made sense. That didn't make much sense either but confronting Him did and for a while that was the only thing that jolted me.

I headed West for a career, man, fortune, new experiences, exotic city, job, fame. I (finally) surrendered my child back to his father, stayed in a commune, ran out of money, had an accident, slept in a truck stop and ended up the year with twice as much money in the bank as when I started. My child returned. Two books are written and a year's experiences accumulated which I could never have gotten without a leap into faith.

XVII

Difficult forgiveness

Even forgiveness comes in levels.

———

I vowed I would hate them and in living that vow, took the responsibility for my own pollution out of a fading memory of a sin and sinner long gone.

———

There was an area where I wholly, utterly in the most microscopic examination could not forgive myself. Waiting, praying, yielding wouldn't do it either until one day I spilled my communion cup and I was kneeling before the First Community Church, Columbus, Ohio, altar. Red juice was on my hands. No way of wiping it. My blouse was expensive. I didn't have a handkerchief and my neighbor didn't see it. Nobody saw it . . . that separated me. At once the liquid was not in my throat or going down my stomach. Redness was on my hands. And "supposings" hit me. Suppose I was there—with Him—and it was His bleeding. Would I not do His bidding even if it meant my own self-forgiveness that He had asked?

Forgiving the man who continued to hurt me was like fighting a battle, and coming home feeling defeated; yet winning.

～～

It happened again in a strange church where a man and his wife were extra friendly, and I was a visitor. He had kept me from a job six years before but I'd forgotten his face. After singing, worshiping and potlucking together inside the church, he reminded me who he was and then, I remembered. But by then, it was too late to hate.

How can you pray and laugh with someone and hate them after the service?

When I became aware of a third and fourth thing like this happening and of situations with others similarly taking place, it became very clear to me that forced forgiveness exists and I was being a part of it. I feel God is a part of it too.

～～

To be worthy of a mission, I must be guarding of time, dedication, willingness to sacrifice desire; even the desire to be close to Him, for the desire to affect His will. The whole thing gets mixed in with forgiveness.

～～

Sometimes forgiving another is unwarranted courtesy. My husband's new wife treated one of my sons with unconcern. I easily constructed hate from this. But why? She had also provided a home for another son and the father, whom she married. I have to be willing to admit the change within myself toward this woman as God takes away my unforgivingness and shows me ways to change. Yet sometimes there's a recall of hate because it feels an awful lot better to me than this new stuff.

Ask forgiveness. Seek. Knock for it. For we know not from what inner battlefields support may come for the victory.

Finally—I forgive you for wearing the scar. I forgive you for displaying the scar. I forgive the wrenchings off of the scab and the bleedings of the scar; the rewoundings you allowed yourself which was nothing but your asking to be punished.

(Hey–do you mean I have to
forgive him for being what he is;
for not being what he could be; for
changing me when I am in his
presence? He doesn't deserve it,
Lord.)

I see "cripples" all around. I hear their cry, their flailings. I sense their anger. I can encircle their anger with my forgiveness, enwrapping their hostilities with my steadiness. I don't always want to. It may be my only mission.

I dropped and injured a child and could not forgive myself unless Christ commanded. Not even then. The answer lay deeper. My sister stopped her reading and looked up at me one night: "Are you better than Christ?" Nonsense. I told her she wasn't thinking. "He had to forgive Himself" was the way that she finally answered me. "Christ forgive Himself?" I didn't like the thought and the "I didn't like" seemed easier to live with than scratching through the kernel of her thinking for its substance. Christ felt. Christ was divine. Christ was human. At times He even cried out, not knowing. When I think about Christ I know that I don't know about His self-forgiving. What I know is this: Making any kind of sense out of our Lord's self-forgiving—if even for a second—makes my self-forgiving markedly easier.

＿ン→ム

XVIII

Willingness—rung five

When we are willing to move out of enslavement, He'll lead. Break with conscious wrong whatever it is—He's there. After nineteen years of a wrong marriage, I got courage enough to break it. He was there. I knew it was His leading. I know it now. That doesn't mean everything went right. It didn't have to. "Right" doesn't mean perfect.

Our first need may be clarification, intensive asking, a chiseling out of the haziness of our thinking what we really want. Then healing follows.

Even as I ask for healing, I am asking in part that I may be healed of the familiarity of being unhealed.

Placing a weak experience in Christ's hands can be the first step in allowing Him (at a future date, in a future way) to make of it something directional. My radio doesn't play at the same volume all the time. Every friendship doesn't exist within the same intensity. I don't always sense Him around me. Sometimes I do.

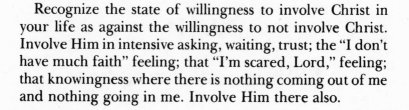

Recognize the state of willingness to involve Christ in your life as against the willingness to not involve Christ. Involve Him in intensive asking, waiting, trust; the "I don't have much faith" feeling; that "I'm scared, Lord," feeling; that knowingness where there is nothing coming out of me and nothing going in me. Involve Him there also.

If you don't have faith, but you want it, pray you may be led to search where it can be found and for the grace to recognize it.

Don't have faith? Start with honesty. Do you or do you not want to be healed? To ask is one thing—to want to be healed, quite another. Then, you get a sensing that healing is taking place, one of the most difficult of all realizations. Why did Jesus pinch-out healings? Why didn't He heal centuries of afflicted for miles by the wave of His hand and get it over with? He seems to have been operating restrained within some law of inner honesty. He kept asking people what they really wanted: if they knew?

And greatly wounded people(He said) were to get forgiven first (they didn't want forgiveness, they wanted to walk). Almost as though He demanded their renewed belief in themselves before He ever got around to patching up bodies. It is pretty hard to know what He had in mind except "Ye *are* the Temple."

There is a sense in which the guy producing the miracle has a right to his own time and method. And the guy waiting for it has an obligation . . . to wait, listen, deepen, be still, observe, stand by, believe, anticipate, rehope, re-expect, be ready to receive. . . .

Looking down, I see the battlefield. One may walk away from the battlefield upward to another level (of livingness) where horror still remains horror, (diversion does not dilute it). But one *has* put distance between; perspective *has* been altered, not removed but added onto. Belowness exists; but aboveness also.

Try this not with a battlefield but with places in your life that still hurt after all these years.

Maybe "Please heal, Lord" means:
I am willing to yield, Lord
- *the desire for continued illness.*
- *the fear I won't be healed.*
- *the fear that his illness will be nasty, will smell, will be repulsive, will drain me.*
- *the fear if he isn't healed, I'll be stuck with his convalescing.*

The surgeon refused to sew the leg until the infection had left. The seeping wound lay open many days. So with Christ? Are we not fix-positioned in our woundings (with His knowing that's where we are) until infection leaves? In our deepest woundings He seems to insist on His timing. Not ours.

Toward instant sewing up of my soul, I always plead. But He heals instead in His season, cell by cell, crumb by crumb. From the inside out. And I must be willing to wait.

XIX

Falling off ladder

All my insides were snarled and stirring and they couldn't find their way back into the tapestry. Loose threads dangled and I took tranquilizers forgetting Christ.

———

Life wastes. My friends all have talents. Most will go unrecognized. A perfect daffodil lay hidden in a field of fire-brush. Same lesson. I can only conclude that fame isn't important. Following is.

———

There is a level of life one touches in intense pain. In futile living. Also loneliness, like an underground pit each of us enters alone. Even in the midst of profitable hurrying, we are occasionally stopped, "pulled" back and down into it. Alone we decide what perspective the pit offers that we will carry upward into other facets of our lives.

XX

Getting back on

Getting Back On
Sometimes it becomes a question of falling down with God or falling down without Him.

Abandon yourself to the will of God moment by moment. Think not of the hour, of the half-hour; think only of the next moment.

Yield wholly to the anxiety and pray that you may be led out of it . . . and wait for the praying to become effective.

Get it out of it . . . and wait for the praying to become effective.

This too, will pass, and in passing, I am to let it pass.

It is not the beatings that scar.
It is the lack of perspective at the time we are lashed, beaten, denounced, denigrated.

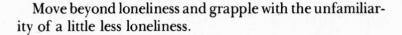

Move beyond loneliness and grapple with the unfamiliarity of a little less loneliness.

Many of us feel unworthy of happiness but okay with pain.

Then we recover and mark time.

More pain.

Jesus said He brought a new way—that we no longer need settle for the familiarity of hurt, but for the strangeness of love.

My ex-husband equated love with food; a man I dated equated love with rejection. He was repelled by my outward affection but came seeking me whenever I was mean and hurting. And for a long time I played the game. I hurt him and he returned. Then one day I fell in love with him and he never came back.

Why do we excuse our grasp of the old rather than fight our way to the new? The old is familiar. Unfulfillment is familiar and pain is familiar. So is failure.

The Easter message is they saw the empty tomb and "were afraid." Resurrection, rebirth, renewal carry fear—the fear of change, leaving the familiar, going from renewal to more renewal and losing the way back to not renewal.

We are rarely freed together. More often, alone. It is the unfamiliarity of uncharted ways that sends us back to the stability of the prison.

One final possession I held onto like a diamond ring—the ashes of past mistakes. Daily I fingered through nineteen years of marriage, loss of job, sale of the house. Depression! Did He want me to give up that possession, too?

~~~

Yieldings are a point of departure as well as a point of arrival. So are healings.

~~~

We were in Wyoming and without a place to live. I was desperate. The crude dwelling on the muddy, snake-infested hillside was no place for a ten-year-old. I had no job. Money was low. Is this where God had led? Days of meditating brought unansweredness and I sought the Methodist church and asked the pastor to pray. He requested our names, where we had come from, wished to go to; gave a quick prayer and ushered me into the hall. Suddenly, I had a nudging to look in a phone book. I called the Full Gospel Business Men's Association. I was soon in the local president's home in a chair with three people's hands on my head and that night we got invited to a prayer cell and potluck at a lake. As the praying grew louder, a couple who knew nothing of our plight invited us into their home to live. They were crying. A few minutes later it started all over . . . "The Lord is telling us to invite them . . ." they said. They thought it was a "nudging"—more a "shove." I thought so, too. We stayed there until another nudge came along, when it seemed, after three months in Casper, the Lord was moving us on.

Remember your job is to yield all. And then to trust. It is your attitude that is important as well as your achievement. Christ will infill the gaps and actively assist in your centering down . . . willingness to . . . motivation toward.

You may have to scrape the bottom of the barrel: "Lord, give me the desire to center." The time-lapse may be a minute, week, year. The Lord deals in slow-realizations. Time is not the same in the stream of the Holy Spirit.

There were 150 students hiking to a four-bedroom house with five beds. They were having a peace march and I felt sympathetic and offered a rest stop. I prayed for help. I was in over my head. Then four women gave their homes the same way. Four more. I ended up with only two guests, and at midnight someone reached us with another empty set of rooms. I no longer felt like the whole, heavy loaf but a piece of yeast that had helped the loaf to rise.

Ministry of Relinquishment
I came to my senses. It isn't how much you relinquish to God or how fast, or when. But, the movement of relinquishment. Is it out of despair? futility? love? hope of gain? a mixture?

XXI

There may not be time to get to the top

Let the dead bury their dead (let the rotting rot).

Most things are mixtures. The command becomes an order to sift through, fork apart, reason by singling out glimpses, separate and segregate. Let me be specific: My mother, age 80, was locked in a corridor babbling but with daily seconds of lucid awareness. Her deadness we had to "salute and pass on" and ignore. Her aliveness we honored.

When the day came she wanted a doll, we bought her one and talked about its clothes. When she was incontinent and strapped in a chair where the nurses had already secured her harness, we touched her hair, her forehead. Then, we left.

Much was in-between—waitingness—transition-ness. Every time we went into the rest home, we had to fork through the same situations all over again . . . what was alive, what was "dead," what in transition.

It was work. It was why seeing her was so difficult. I was constantly picking apart that which was dying, that which would come suddenly alive, and the rest of her personality that was hazily bridging those two. That which was my mother. That which was not my mother. Thought:

"This is the teacher she used to be."

"This is what she is becoming (five months to live)."

71

"Look at what she does today (babbling, playing with doll and doll clothes).

It cost me a lot of energy in my own changingness to allow her to keep on changing. That was work. And I kept myself out of that rest home all I could.

⁂

I've come upon a page torn from my diary. It reads like this: "I felt exhausted seeing mother chawing the harness that ropes her to the chair, clothes askew. I panicked. I ran after three people because I had to find out if her dying were more real or her living . . . was she worse?

One of them, a nurse, said: "No, I wouldn't say so. Your mother's tied so she won't get hurt. But she likes to kick her feet. And she's been chattering happily."

An aide said: "I believe the problem is we have her harness too tight around the chair."

I felt like swimming for shore. It was too much to deal with—her dyingness, her undyingness, the nurses, the harness, the long, locked corridor . . . aides. I raced out of her room to the sunlight. I felt betrayal. Then a cleaning lady stopped me. What she said made sense:

"They took her teeth out. She's shrunk so badly, they can't figure any way to get her teeth to stay in."

⁂

Weeks before she died my mother recognized me and smiled. I sensed in her a total yielding to dying. Complete relinquishment to the process. No anxieties. No guilt. No remorse. And even in her dyingness, I almost envied her yielding.

When she finally died, and I went back to the funeral—to the old childhood streets, the rejecting houses, the hideous school, the frightening corners, a field in which there was a beating (I had remembered) the scab was pulled off. I prayed to get rid of the horror of going back. God took the hurt. But I kept it also.

And then one day a friend said to me: "You can't help the past. You can, the present. You can refuse the crippling attitudes of your father in the *now* of your life. This minute!"

She was right. I couldn't relive my childhood just as I couldn't do anything back in that past but see it horror-filled. To "do" anything else would be the past moving in and taking over things in my present.

Forgiveness may not end with a dying.
  It may begin with a dying.
    There may need to be re-forgiveness
      long after death, over and over and over.
      Not to be kind to the dead.
      To be kind to the living.
        To the person who now moves on . . .
          who must move on.

There are many levels of dying, many levels of living, many levels of abandonment. Maybe all that is needed is a simple striving this very minute for one higher level.

Because a close acquaintance has died, I am terribly alone. Yet when my friend went away to Europe a summer, I was not overcome. We remained out of contact. But when we met again, finally, there was great rejoicing. I think about dying that way too.

Slow dying is a transition for the living—it allowed us a lesser brand of shock than that which is severe. It gave me a chance to feel. I want her to die because she twitches and she's gray. I don't want her to die because she is my mother and it brings my death closer. Her transition is slow—like venturing across the border and going back to this side for more papers, more clearance and then starting across again.

I seemed to be collecting lessons in the five years of her dying that could never have been mine had her death come suddenly, shockingly, unsufferingly. Jesus spoke of the fruit of long-suffering.

There is a suffering of the dying so strung out it makes no sense. Like a spotlight on a stage that nobody needs except it points out something else. In this case it points to Him who is above all suffering, all pain, all joy, all striving, all nothingness, all silence, all emptiness, all unansweredness, all ploddings. Pain and suffering are vehicular. Steps to ascend a summit. Avenues upward. Scaffolding to be ripped down as the mountaintop perspective is gained. So you may say, who wants all this perspective? (Not I, Lord. I don't want it. Who wants to suffer so another may see? Not me, Lord).

Are you willing to surrender your loss?
To ask that He show you how to live without it?
Might it carry a nuance of gain?

74

XXII

God allows wastage/waiting

Why doesn't God start us at the top of the ladder?
God allows wastage. Sometimes His time is spent for years dragging us upward to those mountain clearings from where we can see down, all around, and make choices—or sit there forever in the clearing refusing them.

To learn to wait often means just that—learn!
Yield the desire to not wait. Turn to Christ in a bleeding that is sometimes necessary during waiting. Cry "Lord, help me not to turn against myself."

Waiting means re-noticing . . . (water on the edge of a bud, sunbathed barns; white trees at night). Pretend you know the strength of His arms, the look of understanding present in His eyes. Affirm 100 times a day that He leads you and you are unfolding. Ask Him to be there and know against anything else in all the world it is true. He's there. But you must renotice constantly.

The box is comfortable and stable, today. Feels okay for now. The newness, the freshness, the openness of the hole in the box is frightening. I don't know where it will lead. I don't know which I want.

———✍———

My father used to crank the old Dodge. The rest of us sat in the car in the garage waiting. There was nothing to do but wait. The morning was grey. We sat with our lunches and our books. We couldn't talk. We couldn't leave, or help. We had only one thing to do—wait for the engine to start, to turn over and keep going . . . to churn up enough roaring that the old crank could be put away and the car coasted out of the drive, into motion that would carry us to school on time. I remember that I crossed my fingers and sat on my hands until we got to the school yard and I knew with certainty that that terribly unbearable period of waiting was over.

Years later I faced an operation alone. I had reason to think that I would not return. The giving up of what is familiar and of what has been, the laying down of life in a cold, mechanical room seemed a trip of full madness.

There was a private inner process of disciplining that said: "God is nearby." But, what I was responding to was fear. I felt like a radar screen madly twisting to pick up a beam that someone, some place, cared. I was terribly impatient. The anesthetist stood ready. His grey person gave me no support. Assistants standing by the operating-table seemed duty-bound with nothing for me to work with in that particular situation but hope.

At first I thought God didn't care. But at the same instant I knew He could if He chose. I wondered if this rocky island was what Jesus walked through in His forsakings.

As I thought about this experience and some like it many years later, I began to realize that prayer often involves a change of pace, a slowing downness of living routines. Prayer sharpens perspectives. Reaching-out sharpens awareness-minutes. Not pushes them. Sharpens them. I saw that Jesus probably had to go through a lot of waiting. And knowing this why didn't He speed up the waiting? Why did He pray so long alone without waking somebody up?

Was it to set an example? Or because there was absolutely nothing else He could do as He saw it, using all of His intellect, spiritual closenesses, knowledge of the answers that were needed, but not forthcoming—except pray.

Eventually the praying, the reaching out brings results. Like the old crank on the Dodge. Eventually after all that unhappy effort and after those hour-long minutes of waiting, something happened. Energy collected and drove the car and us to school. But there was nothing, absolutely nothing, that anyone could do for us while father cranked the car—we had to wait!

It is okay to have unbelief for a lot of years. There is a timing to a blossom. Did you ever try to pray open a rosebud?

It is not waiting that is so painful. Our lives are full of waitings—for a baby to be born, for a show to begin, for a three-minute egg to cook, for a war to officially end. It is the wandering around lost inside the waitingness.

Not all minutes of all waitingness can be constructive. Some are. When I think of it that way, I like waitingness better than nonwaitingness.

My son fell out of the tree, but the doctor wouldn't sew him up until he lathered his head with surgical soap and water and cleaned out the wound. *Then,* he got out the needle and the medicine. And the bandages. And started everything healing. First, he removed all infection and that made the wound hurt worse.

He waits until I know that I must do it
  with a tenacity of "mustness" that I'll do it even
    if God doesn't give me a "go" flash or hold back the
      traffic.
  He waits while I writhe
    Until I get my own priorities straight
      in my own sensing—not somebody else's sensing.
    Then, after this is accomplished
      (never, I think without agony)
    do I have the feeling the
      door is opening a crack.

The fluid life takes time. Jesus wept. Jesus walked. I doubt Jesus ran.

Without doubt there are testings in life. Deliberately I was thinking of these on the mountain on which I was hiking. What matters if these (testings) are of God, life, or the mountain? They exist and if we do not pass the test we may remain on a spiritual level beneath where God waits to help us. How many times does He wait while we writhe, our yeast molding within, the bread refusing to rise?

XXIII

Marking time

Marking Time
I noticed another way of praying for someone I hated. To build his prayer bank, a reservoir of prayer, a future field of force.

It disconnected me from him but connected me to his betterment.

I don't know what it did for me. For the moment I felt better.

Threading
When I read *The Cross and the Switchblade,* I realized Wilkerson had to be specific in his intensive askings. His first New York trip had failed. His grandfather said he hadn't expanded his God-reach far enough. There was a threading of the thing he tried and the thing that lay in the future. The God-guidance he misinterpreted and the God-guidance yet to come.

XXIV

Higher healing—higher fear

Higher Healing

Too often we approach one single meeting carrying a bit more joy than necessary; or a bit more fear. Unbalancing. He withholds answers I have noticed in my case sometimes until the inner delicacy of balancing has been restored. I was still very uneasy when I realized uneasiness can be balanced with faith; apprehension with prayer; and fear with humility. God's healing is very often first in proportions in that direction where the balance is off. My countering His efforts to restore my balancing only makes me uncomfortable inside. Then I have another misbalance to redo—my uncomfortableness.

I dare not linger. I must salute and pass beyond to a distance that contributes to my wholeness.

I cannot cure their sickness but I can do something to keep my health.

You were scarred.
   You were beaten.
     But He brought you through.

Can it be? Is it possible? That a part of me had to remain vulnerable to the situation so that another part of me would not be hurt?

He clears the path. Why should I clutter it? He opens the way. Why should I insist on barriers?

Higher Fear
Respect for fear is okay. My other sister is so afraid of sweets that respect for her fear is stronger than her obsession for chocolate cake—and for that reason she's a winner.

The secret is the instant attack. I'll explain. When my sister got respect for one crumb, she began to win. After that she lost twenty pounds.

Ask so you can *receive;* seek to *find*—but do I want that? Am I in a position where I no longer need to fail?

Yesterday I overcame.
 Today I worried.
  That doesn't make me bad.
   It makes me reach out more.

84

(I want to change but not so fast, God. I need to remember who I am for awhile or I'll end up without any friends.)

～～

Dieting can be as much a putter-downer as the over-stuffing. Sex can be as much of a burden as no sex. The image is of me sitting on Me and chasing myself into breathlessness while the word that sparkles is "upgrade." Enough chaos. Enough masochism. Enough beating.

～～

There are times when the only way forward is to give up, give in, without a crutch, another person, a future dream, present despair.

One has to stand ultimately alone.

He *will* lead. He *will* answer. You *will* know.

～～

How many times did men closely associated with Jesus slip into sinking sand? One might imagine that living in proximity to God's Son, they had the world by the tail. Radiant! Maybe. But, I think a forced labor came first. I think it got easier only when they told themselves over and over and over they couldn't make it alone; a journey with Him would be different only after they got down on their knees.

Your duration of belief is not always the same. Jesus said "Never be afraid." "You are worth more than a sparrow." "Believe me. Let them not frighten you." "Happy is the man who never loses faith in me." You can't always believe in the same intensity even if the information comes from deep within that you "should." Many positions of belief are available. If you're stock-still in one get out.

Practice sit-ups. Have you forgotten how your muscles respond the more you sit-up?

———

As the wind blew they cried, "Master, Master, we are about to die."

Jesus: "Where is your faith?"

Wasn't He saying "Of course your faith escapes. This is the human condition. Get it back"?

———

There is such a thing as reducing numbers in order to be gathered.

Numbers of voices, obligations, worries, calories, expenditures, minutes lost, conversations.

———

Didn't the twelve have power to make other people listen to them if they had power to raise the dead and cure lepers?

Couldn't they infuse a lesson? Inject a lesson? Transfuse a quart of strong, powerful instruction?

Why didn't they?

I lost my billfold. Later in the day I found it. It lay underneath the car seat. That which I needed I should have known was there all along. Another lesson.

Those fishing experts toiling an empty night must have felt like a bunch of exhausted fools when Jesus asked them to believe in the unbelievable and lower their nets still one more time into the thrashing sea—in overfatigue, disbelief, and numbness. But take note!

All of this went *before* the miracle of the big haul of fish.

Maybe it was all necessary—in that order—the over-fatigue, disbelief, numbness, thrashing sea and feeling fools.

In dying a little today, I can die in far greater amounts, far easier, tomorrow.

Who wants to play a part in his own healing? Yet didn't Jesus encourage it?

There is a sacrificial fifteen-minute prayer which doesn't ask anything but merely holds another up. You are sacrificing because you don't feel like holding him up but like holding yourself up.

Get rid of distractions. Go to your mountain and start up. Of course you are going to miss some things along the way. But what is more important—the balmy breezes you are leaving, or the climb?

―――

Only by reaching my own self-disgust, staying in it and feeling it, could I work it through. Like the hysterectomy. I had to go through it myself.

―――

There are times when it is good to accept on faith. But there are times when it becomes terribly important to know. I dreamed about my son somewhere in Alaska, said a prayer about his plight, but got busy, ran down his address, dispatched a check and letter special delivery. It takes both.

―――

It is more clear and inescapable to me: Christianity promises burdens, not companionship. You may suffer and die in aloneness. You may be unable to explain it. Or find anyone to explain it to.

XXV

The way up is work—
the way in, more so

Don't get stopped at the first level of your aloneness. Let it
wear, agonize, pulsate, throb but lean not on the stability of
your agony lest you become numbed. Take one brief, fleet-
ing, innocuous, insignificant step beyond aloneness. This is
your new point. And every new point must have its beginning. Some things can emerge only if we are still.

Some things emerge only if we are purged.

Some things can emerge only after I let go.

Open-living promises only the chance to demand of
yourself that you live in that awful openness. It may mean
that like Schweitzer, you lay aside talent for a shovel and a
hoe. That you will not be understood

    Or accompanied;

    Noticed;

    Admired, liked or spared.

Evelyn is a baker in a Casper, Wyoming country club.
One morning she went out to the lake to the country club
kitchen to bake bread. She thought she brought a new cake
of yeast. But all she had was a speck that wasn't enough to
raise a thing except another yeast speck. Yeast by yeast,
speck by speck—all one lonely morning while everyone
slept. The bread-rising miracle was nowhere in her life.
Evelyn's job was to multiply the yeast. Otherwise she would
be dealing forever with nothing more than a pile of crumbs.

Who cares if you win only by an inch in the last race in the afternoon. It's the winning that counts. I was on an airplane. I lost my sandwich only it didn't hit the seat; I caught it at the under-edge of my drop table, a pickle landing solely in my lap. The man next to me sighed. "That's all that matters," he said. "You caught it." That same year the doctor said my wounded son might lose his leg. He didn't. He went back to school and the coach started him running. The coach made him mad, hurt his feelings, let him ache. The coach wouldn't let him quit. A sophomore, he came in second, won his letter, won over the pull toward a losing. The winning counted more than the fact he almost didn't win.

XXVI

Emergency ladder

Emergency Ladder
Unclench a fist and let go of that which is precious for one moment. Do not say "I will let go" or "I can let go" but "I am letting go now."

Don't be afraid to crawl inside and wait.
To do less until direction comes.
To make a decision not to make a decision.
To promise yourself nothing but the hurt
Until the hurt heals.
Let the deep hurt, hurt you deeply
until it releases you.

Do something meaningful until the adjustment has taken place. By the time you've accomplished this, the changeover will have been complete. Even for an hour's drudgery. Try to locate the meaningful and let the adjustment take care of itself.

Step into the imbalance. Everything doesn't have to balance. Fainting isn't so bad either if it comes to that. Coming out of it alone can be. But now you're dealing with aloneness, not fainting.

Read the Bible for dialogue.
Talk to someone about Jesus.
Put the problem in God's hands.
And a kind arm around yourself.

There is always further prayer as a means of correction.

But prayer and wishing do not close all gaps. (It is not necessary that all gaps be closed. One strong bridge over a river is sometimes all that is required.)

Of course you "love" a person. We can't drop our emotions onto lamp posts. There will be another at a later intersection farther on and another and another . . . farther on and farther on. . . .

What you need is faith the Holy Spirit can work through you right now to achieve the next minute's transition.

Sometimes a relationship ends like the shattering of glass. And we are left receiving—not from the relationship but from the shattering—the shock, the suddenness, the abruptness of change.

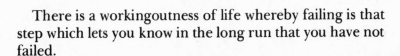

(Replace costumes, cars, husbands and states, jobs, friends, dreams. But always there remains He who started to guide you in the first place.)

Your humbling which is at the center of your suffering is your seeding, budding, living wholeness; fertile soil where your green shoots of renewal are already under way.

Get in a position of expectation. You don't need answers as much as a willingness to wait for answers. And a faith in reaching out that you'll be given the faith supply that is needed to wait for their arrival.

There is a workingoutness of life whereby failing is that step which lets you know in the long run that you have not failed.

I need to commit myself; burn the bridges of the last minute. Go forward to the next minute expecting.

Sometimes you can long so much that the only means of living for the hour is to deeply release, wholly relinquish, totally abandon the merest suggestion of a thought of . . . the person . . . you desire.

So often the steadying stillness of another who understands is enough. All that is needed within that steadying stillness may be to know one can remove familiar fears and go on in a raw vulnerability—but go on.

Some things are tolerable only when treated as temporary.

Sometimes you cut away to restore. Have you forgotten?

And have you forgotten that life is the acquisition of many things, but not people?

XXVII

Knowings, quickenings, promptings

Sometimes an experience one day has an altogether different appearance awaiting dissection—say a week away. Which was right? Maybe both. They are progressions of knowing.

There are levels of understanding, stages of enlightenment within the same experiencing. The deepest meanings may come at a time when there is a quietness without to receive the knowings that surface from within. Maybe ten years beyond.

I feel I have gotten so much from bits of conversation splattered over great spans of time. One answer was 100 words spread out over ten years and I had to fork back into several scenes and several conversations to retrieve this "knowing." After I hooked onto it, lifted it out and pieced into what triggered it last week, then I had a diamond—a gem that started me unraveling the present, not disguising it. But the answer took ten years, like hearing someone stutter in pieces of sentences over 120 months. And it finally came to me from different things lots of people said to me. Finally I packed it all together.

Each food carries one dominant flavor; so each relationship. When I was young, I noticed one of my aunts had a drawer full of bracelets. She slept in a large bedroom with a fireplace and a great dresser with a drawer full of different colored loops she wore on both of her arms. Everything centered around that. She didn't marry; she taught school, wrote letters. Bracelets were her dominant flavor. And since then it has been true of everyone I have had any "acquaintanceship" with or come to know. A dominant impression arrives with each person and my awareness of him.

Knowings can seep at you through silences. Promptings often through conversation. Quickenings from anyplace.

A man came to me very shaken. He needed to talk about a marriage splitting up and in talking, fell in love. Then I realized I must respect his sufferings and protect myself from his writhings for they were his, not mine.

I could not be his answer. I could be an oasis and this is sometimes enough. I had to make him move on.

In so many ways a spiritual experience is like a friendship. There need be no high level of communication. Trust exists in a friendship; fadings in and out; good feelings across great distances for many years. I speak with my friend via phone and letter. I need not hear his voice every hour. Or once a week. I need not speak to him of every wish. He knows. In a thousand ways we communicate through currents of understanding that only need to be recognized. They exist already.

A package of strange circumstances over a few weeks may be God saying "Now, don't lose heart. Don't get discouraged."

A big museum in Columbus, Ohio refused to give me a large historical document that I felt nudged to research and write on. It existed no other place and I decided against finishing the piece because I was stopped dead. A year later, I went to a Quaker retreat in Cleveland and, arriving ahead of the others, crossed the backyard to a strange building and went inside. It was the Western Reserve Society Museum. They had the document, gave me a borrower's card and said "Help yourself." I felt connected to God and to the place as well and to the piece He seemed to be instructing me to write.

Work For The Night Cometh
In the dark, lonely church in the season after Christmas, enwrapped in despair, I went to the altar, to a white-draped cross and knelt. A mechanical device was playing holiday

music and amplifying it beyond the glazed fields, the darkened freeway. It was then that I asked my mission of God and His timing as well. I remember that twice in the next few minutes I was utterly shaken. And I wouldn't have been if the hymn that was playing hadn't stopped mid-sentence when the light in the record player dimmed to a red pinprick. The needle arm stilled in mid-air.

It must have been three or four minutes before I got the message . . . and by then the lesson was clear. "Time is urgent. (For) timers do go off, pieces do get stopped midscore, hymns do remain half-sung, people kneel and never rise. It was almost too much.

XXVIII

The handgrips—Christ

Over and over He seemed to be saying:
"Ye are the temple. Love yourself.
Believe that ye *are* the temple."

Jesus made people decide what they wanted, put it into
words, think it out, express their ambivalence. There was a
man blind by the roadside who shouted. People in front of
him told him to hold his tongue. He called out all the
louder. "Son of David, have pity . . ."
Jesus asked: "What *do* you want me to do for you?"
He asks us that also.

(And there is nothing keeping me from committing my
life whether I am given relief in the quantity in which I
desire it or not).

Christ's appeal was for honesty.
"If any man among you seem to be religious and bridleth
not his tongue but deceiveth his own heart, this man's
religion is vain" James 1:26.

Honesty is exceedingly costly. I wonder sometimes if I am listening in on what is going on inside of me. What thrashing and moaning that I turn my back on and quiet myself with pretense and illusion, deceiving, not Christ, deceiving me.

The Apostles
They complied. They followed, they yielded, they obeyed, but only after they allowed themselves to be convinced even a crumb's worth. Christ tries a million ways to make us see without *making* us see. To relook at who He is. Who we are.

(Suppose Jesus had slipped up and the last of those hungry 5,000 on the hillside would have grumped home, starved. Would that last guy have discovered miracles with a Lord who fed not 5,000 but 4,999. And let the story go down through the centuries unedited?)

Christ's freeing brings a rearrangement. Reassessment. Probably relocation, also.

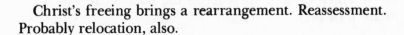

Did you notice that Jesus involved others. "Stretch forth your arm." "Arise, take up your bed." He was the healer, why didn't He do it all by Himself?

He was the convincer, too. (Believe in me. Believe in yourself. Believe in praying, in waiting, in yielding, in emptiness that comes before plenty; in nothingness that comes before enlightenment.)

———

Sometimes He makes me taste, enfold, entrust, feel and live with every solitary crumb of my going-forwardness, my groping onwardness, my reachingoutness.

———

Seeking, asking, demanding, believing, hoping, permeating every pulsation with prayer. Remember that He kept it up all night. Why did He pray all night if not "So, also shall ye." I think He was desperate in His non-connectedness, His reaching-to-God-ness. (So, also shall we? because so, also are we?)

———

Christ's method of healing asked something of three people—himself, God, the one being healed. Stretching forth one's hand, running to tell the priest, standing up. Even covering one's eyes with mud. Surely healing was not dependent on these gestures. Christ must have believed in involvement as against dispensation of blanket-healings. Not "I heal you" or "My father heals you" but *your* faith has made you whole."

All the paralytic wanted was his legs.
But Jesus said: "Your sins are forgiven."
Where does it say that the paralytic figured he hadn't been
heard?
Or that forgiveness was the first dose of Christ's "medicine"?

For that matter why didn't He bombast a miracle? Pollute miracles? Dynamite the crowds with berserk miracles? Why didn't He make those 5,000 stoop over and pick up 80,000 baskets of fish instead of twelve? Why didn't He bomb His voice so its waves could be picked up centuries later in TV studios—so people wouldn't have to come seeking Him so far from where He is? He could have cleaned up all the devils in one swoop over the cliff. Why did He piecemeal His job? Maybe if He threw the book at us, we would rely on His "throwing," His miracle-making stuff, instead of listen-ings, waitingness, receptivity.

I prayed for a boy in my elementary school library who hated my stories. Desperation brought me to putting my arm around him and I found I couldn't help myself. While I read to the rest of the children, I noticed my inside yielding to the outside of the child I previously disliked. I don't know where Jesus was that day. I suspect in my library.

With all the humanness of Christ, I am guessing that He might have had a fear, too, of nonrecognition, urgency, being forsaken, dying, being misquoted, misunderstood, unpublished, unfulfilled, unloved. His humanness makes my humanness less surprising.

XXIX

Longings—rung six

I bleed in my longings. I become very quiet. No answers.
Only crumbs.

Today, the spiritual part of me is satisfied. My friend and
I spiritually met. But, the physical me wants a package of
recognitions that say "I touch," "You are," "I feel," "You
know me," "You're here," "I'm here," "Close in," "Reas-
sure." "Leave no empty space between us."

Needs do not always need to be met. Centering is sometimes all that counts.

All needs do not have to be met with the structure of what
we might call permanency. The fluid state is always in battle
with the granite package.

I loved a man but he gave me back too little.
Yet this made my cup none the less full. It still overflowed.
There is strength and vitality to overflowing.
I am not free to demand a package to cure my loneliness.
I must live in my loneliness—and in my loneliness, overflow.

The love-need-wound . . . expressing itself in sex, smoking, food, etc., is literally lessened when I am simply acting-reacting spontaneously. I think this says a lot.

In therapy:
I am beginning to think of life in terms of the times when I don't hurt inside.

When someone isn't ripping off the scab and I have to run around to find something to heal over the wound again.

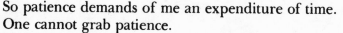

The hurt exists on one level. Blessings on another. That doesn't make the hurt any less hurting. I notice the hurts *along with* the blessings. But it is the "along with" in life so often that keeps us going, with our heads clear.

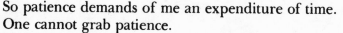

So patience demands of me an expenditure of time.
One cannot grab patience.
How many of the things that I try to snatch are in the final analysis . . . given?

Locking the doctor out doesn't save you from a ruptured appendix. Lock him out if you want to, but unlatch the window. Most of us need Him sometime. And at this point any half-way church attendance might be okay. It is a road in.

And that's what's important—a road in.

XXX

Releasings—rung seven

The great, risky, tricky art of daily, hourly, second by second release.

My releasing you is the leavening—the yeast without which the bread of our relationships may never rise.

It is not necessary to love all in a person always every minute of all times.

Sometimes it is the bit, the crumb, that you adore that far outweighs the unlovable parcel.

———

There is a time to forget (think less often) of another person. But there are different ways of forgetting. Some heal—some scar.

I am to forget Bob in a spirit of trust . . .
  in a spirit of yielding . . .
  in a spirit of trustful yielding.
Which is different than forgetting in anger.
  retaliation
  Martyrdom.

———

I am not to be a collector of anything
  of friendships
  of love affairs
  of writing penpals

I am to release and let go
knowing the lessening of
grasping.
The open, gripless yield.

~~~

Six years after divorce, I was still using the words: "father of my little boys." Suddenly, my psychiatrist pointed out "He is not the father of your little boys." He is the husband of another woman and they are not little boys, they are grown men who need to fall and to be jarred (scarred?) or they'll never rise."

~~~

Once in Washington I saw a vine on the National Gallery of Art. It was so overgrown that it stretched a great wall. But the wall seemed to hold it up easily. As though the vine were saying: "I can afford to exude beauty for I do not have to struggle every inch of the way myself. I have found that which can support a part of me."

~~~

The effort to release must be repetitious over and over, against harmony, against inner accord, bringing discord; the discord of releasing.

~~~

I unclench one finger and I let go of that which is momentarily precious; precious for the moment. It starts with the unclenching of one finger.

All acquaintanceships do not always have to continue. Nor do all churches, every society, most dreams, many plans. Disengagement and dismissal are as real to life as engagement and encounter.

Imbalances are less bad if one is kneeling. "Enter into my deprivation, Lord," Say it over and over and when something begins to release you, say it again.

I had lunch with the man I divorced. It brought mixtures of apprehension, uneasiness, lack of confidence, fear, but in a new proportion of balance not present when we separated five years before. I tried praying while we ate. Neither went down very well. It accomplished nothing except to know that it is the mix of the feelings within us that carries more importance sometimes than the actual encounter that is the current that carries along the feelings. That's all. I have a lot yet to work through regarding him.

Prayer went to work in my son's brain operation. So did handing him over. But it took a whole day of the one to achieve the other.

Give back to God the last minute for reinforcement. Get down on your knees and give back to Him; and in His keeping the hour you have just spent will be an opening into another section of time with Him; better moment; better hour.

When a plane takes off, the mobile steps that got you into the cabin are no longer needed. My mother "told" us that deep unhappiness was the best we could expect in life. After we left her house we went out and found our own. Twenty years later my psychiatrist told me I sought men given to tantrums. At this point I knew I was sick.

Adulthood means putting away the "toys" of childhood, even beatings, if that's what happened. Now, I began asking God to help me. Prayer meetings. Prayer partners. Altar calls. When I knew I was getting better, I sensed movement toward the Lord every time I asked Him to give me more and more of myself and less of my past. When I was fifty, I put my life in His hands at the Pleasant Valley church outside of Chillicothe. Not reasonably. Not like a martyr. Just telling Him again and again, like everybody in the tiny church was doing, to make me a channel. That's when things began to happen. I had one son, no job and an apartment costing fifty dollars a month. But things were beginning to make sense. I no longer needed those "steps"—those attitudes from childhood. In a very real way I felt I was beginning to "take off."

XXXI

Levels of pain—rung eight

Awareness
> As the sea does not pause
> but falls incessantly
> to rise.
> So, awareness

Ah—but there are layers of freedom for which Christ sets us free. Being free to be you is one.

How did you get out of your horrible childhood except that it hurt so bad? Had it hurt less you would have settled for it and closed up and stayed closed.

The Bible says,
"He who brings the sacrifice of thanksgiving. . ." .Sacrifices are not easy. Am I to change my image of "thanksgiving"? What about a hard, difficult thanksgiving?

"You can transmute the energy of bleeding into writing, of running into riding, of weeping into praying. But you may have to get down on your knees to do it."

I have decided.
I want to take off the cloak of past pain even though it is mine and I earned the right to wear it, and reach for the good things I have a right to also.

XXXII

Handing it over

Participatory healing. I had to bleed, trust, wait. Others prayed. The surgeon operated. Isn't this often the way Jesus healed—this mix?

~~~~

In 1949 I was sexually involved and thought I was pregnant. I knelt by my bed in a rooming house in shame and guilt. Suddenly I stopped. "Someone" was in the room. The next day I stumbled around trying to pray away worry but I didn't pray it away—it came back. I pretended a picture of Christ in my bedroom but it got fuzzed over and not clear. Two days later I tried a wobbly faith-risk, wiping out the relationship that had led me where I was. I broke off the engagement. Christ leads us in many steps in knowing until many knowings beyond we trust our lives to Him. It was my first experience in risk.

~~~~

If Jesus could feed 5,000 with a handful of fish could he not have performed better with more? Dried a few? Frozen a few? Why didn't He keep some out for himself in case something backfired?

I waited twenty years for a concert. When the night approached, the theater had only fifteen dollar tickets or "standing in the lobby" until the music began. I nearly took the risk of standing when something restrained me. I prayed "If you want me to go, God, open the way." Then I laid down in my night clothes, went to sleep and the phone rang. It was the box office. Two last-minute seats were unclaimed. I slipped into clothes, raced downtown, arrived after the crowd which was seated for the overture. The seats were fifth row, first aisle, the best in the house.

Stepping aside takes self-belief—to become a bystander and let another (God) work within the situation you have just removed yourself from.

God leads through yieldings, underlinings, restrainings, quickenings, promptings, nudges. But—hold to a position of belief. *Hold!*

Have you thought how much the standby activities of our lives nourish the inner strength of another? By denial to my angry son, I support his house of supply, and so stand by in the background while he jabs at roots; and, finding them, pulls the sweetness of growth marvelously up into his own body for his own nourishment.

Christ said if you have faith as a mustard seed you shall move mountains. That didn't mean with a shovel a mile away. There's something to be said for closeness and bulldozers. Very often I find the mountain won't come to me; I have to go to it.

Then, when I get to the mountain, helpless with my teaspoon, I forget to put in a bulldozer-appeal. Sometimes He sends one anyway; other times it appears I'm to work with only a toothpick because I forgot to ask.

Like old rags, we finger them—familiar worries and gigantic, rich fears. My aunt had a beautiful wig in a box in a trunk she had kept a long time. Then she died and we had to get it all out and examine it in the light. Amazing. It was full of worms. Our worries and fears get too old too, but we keep them, worms and all.

XXXIII

Ascending

God won't play Top Sergeant. I can't fold my hands and wait for orders. He waits to know what I think, how fast I want to move, how much I am willing to sacrifice.

―――

Lot's wife turned around and you know what happened. There is no turning back. Only a pushing through.

―――

When I first started putting these thoughts down, I tried to get into "super-answers"—the forceful, unexpected "loaded" responses that occasionally burst forth. Later I went through a purging and came up realizing that micro-inchings more aptly describe my Christian growth. Like twisting through a forest, lifting one thorn-vine at a time with no footpath visible—with merely a knowledge of where one has been by a glance at the foliage one has somehow managed to walk through. God allows us tangleweed to learn that we can be unsnarled; that we will be hopelessly entwined in the stranglement but that life is for God to give back to us. Progress too.

117

There must be a hurting, bleeding, level of abandonment in which I must live my life to make it worthwhile—and I must let God infill the emptinesses.

—∿—

Yet we must battle for minutes for it is there we win or lose. He is your help *this* minute. Give Him a chance *this* minute.

—∿—

(Why must you give me the full table, God when I so willingly conceded to the crumb?)

—∿—

(Why must I be tossed on so many waters I care so little about?)

—∿—

Occasionally Christ lets us laugh as we ascend. The air hostess forgot my martini, served it as we were landing. I gulped it down. Fifteen minutes later on the ground, I ran into two men I thoroughly hated, responsible for taking my job eight years before. In a vague and fumbling way I remembered hating but it wasn't such an acid remembering. After we'd been talking and acting nice to each other for fifteen minutes, I remembered they deserved to be ignored. But it was too late. Too late to rehate. Does Christ force forgiveness? And with martinis?

Certainly Jesus understands it is rare not to hate, unreal
not to fear, impossible never to judge.
"But there's a point beyond," He seems to say.

Sometimes I tell my son what to do with his time. Other
days we fork through his ideas, and try mine before we
decide. It's sometimes like that with God. Some days His
ideas, some days, mine; some days, a combining.

"Follow me" is not a beginning command. It comes at the
end of a long road of testings. Or, not at all. Until after
death.

My friend had a survival marriage. 1 was divorced. We
went to the woods. I hugged trees. She cooked bacon and
eggs. We did it, keeping silent. Suddenly I watched a bowl
of wet eggs go into a pan of half-fried bacon while she
pointed me to a seat and dished up liquid. I looked franti-
cally for a scrap of paper and finding a towel, I penned,
"Can't it be a little more cooked?" Laughter! We got up and
went home. We had come without salt or cookstove fuel,
pencils or paper and so disorganized it all became laughter
so nourishing with our silence we now became filled.
Ridiculous—that the Holy Spirit provides a meal having
nothing to do with food.

(I'm not so sure He convinced the twelve equally—yet the twelve pivoted their twelve growth levels around Him. And that was all that was important.)

To grow beyond your "growth" you have to step back into the open pain of living, retreating, advancing, trying, failing, bleeding, rising . . . again and again and again.

Maybe it is necessary to forgive and reforgive until it blends into something that has to do with overall forgiveness of which each of us is part.

(It is the hanging on part of resentment that drains me. Not the resenting flash of instant superficial resentment. That's honest. It's the letting-go-chain. After I let go of the fear of letting go, I realize that very often I am asked only to release.)

There is a never-known second at which the last link in the chain begins to collapse, at which the tenacity of resistance of the metal begins to wobble around.
There is a split second which lifts the gull.
A single second when unawareness loses its grip.
A single second when faith becomes stronger than fear.

Churches in southern Ohio are small and intimate and I joined one. So what makes it different? People praying not that my burden may be lifted but that I may continue to bear it without asking to lay it down.

"Reach for the higher things and I will show you an even more perfect way."
The very reaching lessens the hold one had on the former position until, with more graspingness on the higher ledge upward, the new plateau is gained.

I have to be willing to climb up 100 times without reaching the summit and let the mountain pull me back, experiencing the up and down, the height and slippage, until the mountain itself seems enthralled to heave me crestward.

(Give Christ a chance to work. Die little deaths all along the way. Work up to bigger ones. Let your agony point you to the center—not take you away from it.)

"In *my* time" is much more difficult than "In *my* way."
On that brink point of "hatching" we go through the cycle again and again . . . fall, bruise, rise, walk, fall, bleed, wait,

rise, fall . . . over and over. I call it suffering. Most of us do. But in His perspective, I sometimes wonder if these are not the crumb-like steps which we may take or not take. Yet still never lose His love and concern.

God leads through many testings and many trials until trusting (us) with larger crosses. I stopped at a little cross. I didn't want a big one. Bonhoeffer, on the other hand, was tried and tested by God for many years before he was entrusted to give his life. So, I believe God, finding us worthy, grants bigger tasks. Without question, Jesus went to little crosses before the big one.

When God closes doors, He may be saying "Focus." Maybe He's asking for listening or just to "feel" His presence. Or for a chance to lead instead of being pushed, prodded, poked, begged, thought about, forgot about, bribed.

Do not be afraid to notice as you move farther into holy obedience, God treating you as a graduate student. Not a new set of rules but a new interpretation of the old ones.

(Pour yourself out toward love. Do not suck its image toward you.)

(Man 4999 in the feeding of the 5,000 must have given up a thousand times before he got his.)

—————

(Sometimes it is not important to know, but only to follow; Christ had no secretary.)

—————

I look at the miracle once again. It takes time to produce a miracle. There must have been a long waiting period on that hillside before someone got around to Man 4999. He must have felt moods changing watching everyone else eating. (Some pretty shady characters getting miraclized first.) There is no record his courtesy in waiting increased his reward—not in substance nor in recognition. No double fish came his way. He didn't go down in history. Nor ever will. (If I'd have been him, I'd have stuffed my pockets with whatever remained and called it just due.)

With all this supposition, it appears God asked of him the ridiculous, "Wait while the rest go first." The inevitable question was, "Why?"

I can't see that it made any difference whether he did or he didn't, except for one possibility: maybe he'd figured out that God had picked him out for a job to do, and however ridiculous, there was the job!

—————

Remembering the agonies that led ultimately to divorce (like opening myself again to my own resuffering)—

For a long time I tried to dodge this remembering to give myself a palliative. Then I learned to embrace the imbalance, not to try to make things balance. Allow imbalance. Let Christ infill.

And to give Him time. (That time may be a minute, a second, crumbs of release, an hour of repair, a night of aloneness when only daylight offers any semblance of help.) Finally, I wasn't asking to be made better, happier, unresentful, whole. I was asking for His Presence.

XXXIV

Restraining

Restrainings exist.

I had been going to a country church when one Sunday as I was getting up, a restraining came (like a force that wasn't a force at all, holding me back from getting there on time).

I debated and then it got too late.

So, I dashed next door from my apartment to a church I had never been inside and hadn't particularly thought I'd ever enjoy going in.

That day a new group was meeting—Parents Without Partners—and I met a handsome man, a minister, unmarried, and got from the group a calendar of events to take my eleven-year-old son to, and some events for me.

I'm doing nothing to force recognition of restrainings now, but that day I was in the middle of one. It was all about me. It was impossible to have been unnoticing.

XXXV

No answers—rung nine

The No-Answer Prayer
"Lord, I must have help. I cannot go on. Please find me
someone who will care." There was no answer. But God was
waiting with me until the answer came.

The most we get sometimes are clearings. I cried three
hours. Then, a clearing in the forest of my thoughts—as
though He were saying: "Now, then—arise. Go forth listening."

There is a relationship wholly nourishing within ourselves, making friends with ourselves. God insists, demands, refuses to budge some days until I find this self-
love—relationship.

(I feel unwilling to let in His perspective. I have insisted on keeping Him out because my unchangingness comforts / me today.)

◢◣◤

Let the dead bury their dead—let the tormented keep their torment. He did at times.

◢◣◤

Pray for understanding. Often we ask, seek, knock but then crawl back and pull down the antenna. The only way Christ can get to us is shock-action.

◢◣◤

But then at times a faint suggestive strand of His care seems merely, simply, a gentle hand on my shoulder holding me back. I've noticed a rhythm to His restraining and not-restraining, something like our dance teacher who was teaching the waltz, and pushing in on my shoulder blade got me to slow down.

◢◣◤

Sometimes it's like God has gone off on a vacation someplace. I know I'll hear and that He loves me. But He's not around in high awareness. (And what, I ask myself, is so wrong with low awareness? I don't have sadness without my friend's postcard across the ocean every day. I know he remembers me. And the traveler will come back someday.)

"You're doing okay. Don't stop," may be all that God is trying to get across in the underlinings and flickerings this morning.

＞ルﾚ

I don't always have to see my friend with my eyes wide open. I hear her voice in the school hall. I sense her movements. I smell her perfume. By all these hookups I know she's someplace in the school library and if I take different perspective and glance a different direction, I'll see.

Many different ways of realizing the Holy Spirit exist but are difficult to get into words.

And words some days are all I have to work with.

＞ルﾚ

Praying sometimes brings fuzzy answers. The four words "say what you want" may be what Christ is expressing a great deal of the time when we're getting no feedback at all.

Christ, waiting. Waiting with nothing happening. Waiting with nothing happening until we decide what we want.

A spiritual experience is not always a package. It is a tendency toward; a closeness in the midst of . . . a directional tug in some new way where no direction existed before. Even half of a choice which will not link up with the second half of the choice until many years beyond.

I used to demand God answer immediately. What I found instead were moments. Moments that led toward more lucid moments, now directional. I had to keep working with this.

We know God allows suffering. Why? Is it merely a hands-off policy precluding any effort of God to puppet us through our transitions? More and more I sense that God waits while we turn fashionably away. Or (turn) pragmatically away. Or experimentally away.

That His waitingness is His greatest gesture of belief in one tiny life-form that can turn toward Him or turn from Him—took years of non-listening, disbelieving, on my part.

I should have known then what I believe with all my heart today. He supports our full destiny sufficiently to wait great stretches of years—great agonizing years. Restraining rather than interfering. Enduring the risk of losing us entirely. Many times He does lose. But when we find each other (He, us—we, Him) it is worth every hair-wisp of gropingness, every granule of agony which got us there.

Even as He suffers watching our sufferings, this price is His price. He's willing to pay to have us desire to be close to Him. Willingly He loses us until willingly we find Him.

Some endings are good fertilizer. Killing dreams can be okay. The plant lives when the seed dies. If you bury a dream, more expansive dreams may rise up out of the fertile soil—the soil your dream helped fertilize.

XXXVI

Underlinings

Underlinings

One Sunday a minister said "Go forth in fear and trembling." On Monday in another city at a gravesite my aunt said to me: "All you can do is carve your life in fear and trembling." And the same words came back to me again in a book I was reading. After these occurrences, I had no other choice but to keep going and try harder.

—⟩⟨⟨

I read a story to the sixth grade about a water buffalo and the school secretary chatted at lunchtime about hunting in British Columbia. That night my mother lay slowly dying. The minister talked to me about forgiving my dead father and dying mother. Beyond—on the table were four magazines. Old copies. One was a picture of the mountains of British Columbia and one, a water buffalo. Was it Christ saying "I understand. I know what you are going through. I'm with you"?

XXXVII

Transitions

Fear not, for I have redeemed you. When you walk through the waters, I will be with you; and through the rivers, they will not overwhelm you, and through the fire, you will not be burned in the flame. It will not consume you . . . (you'll be singed at times though. And you'll choke in the water. And be unaware of His presence. And all life for awhile will be water and fire.)

It's a shock to go through a transition. And you know you're going to want to turn back. Don't. Keep loosening.

Some days my faith is like teaspooning the sea.
The waves could sweep me in while I'm trying to locate my teaspoon.

Once I went to a retreat. I became very attracted to a young man, much younger than myself—by twenty years. We could do nothing about it. The sexual pressure was very bad. I felt guilt. All the people were older and they were happily married and trying to be good Christians. I was trying, also. But desire got in the way. I went for a walk to try to understand. I came onto a path up a hill and stepped on a dead snake.

My roommate said: "It is not the snake that counts. It is the balance. There is the Holy Spirit and there is the snake, which predominates?"

Out of the retreat came lessons still unfolding in their meaning ten years later. The snake was horrible and I was horror-filled. But the balance of my experience—the part that really counted—was that Jesus Christ, whose new presence I felt, was trying to tell me things about myself I could not believe. That men were attracted to me; that after six children, I still had sexual desire; that I could pray away some pressures but some I had to agonize with; and that prayer, not even somebody else's Christian praying, could wipe them out. But mostly, that He miraculously understood every bit of this.

Jesus dealt a lot with transition
   "The girl is not dead, she is sleeping."
   (The transition had been small—not big.)
   Transition living is the hardest. We lack faith in His promises, but also faith in His Presence. Our level of faith begins often to fall when we have no strong assurance we are not out on a sandbar, alone.
   Getting up off the ground after such an occurrence, one

realizes there are many stages of transition. When the judge said "divorce granted" I had six sons, an old car, debts, no work.

One day an answer dropped into my tracks. A new job. The life on the other side of transition may bring promise. It seemed to for me.

And for that reason, transition for transition's sake is no place to stop. It is something to get on with and to get through.

XXXVIII

Repositionings

There is a natural arrival of shadings at the end of a sequence of bold strokes.

~~~

Yieldings can be a point of departure. I went through a seven-month shredding; job loss, clothes stolen, rejection of friends, exploitation, money loss, car gone.

A part of me died too, a relinquishing in which there can be no return. There are dyings in repositionings that are frightening. And unending.

I noticed God not with me.

Yet, He brought me through. The waters did not inundate or overflow. Or destroy.

They brought me a repositioning. Some repositionings take seven months.

One son got married at seventeen, another got a scholarship. Another went to Alaska, one to the Air Force, another to live with his father. I had only one son with me and then I got a job with much travel and new experiencing. Afterward I noted a small Ohio town where my sister lived— Chillicothe. I wanted to write. I wasn't remarried, hadn't a job, but I found a strange church where everyone prayed for everyone else at the altar. I felt stronger than ever in my life. A clearing. The whole thing seemed like a repositioning, yet it had taken fifty years. Now what?

—⁓⁓

Sometimes we must spare others the travail of trying to cross bridges they cannot cross because of information they cannot have and sensitivities they have not yet known.

—⁓⁓

Often the kindest move is to move not at all. The other will move. Seek his own wounding. Seek his own bleeding and seek his own healing. While it is healing that counts, one must permit another's self-wounding to allow his self-healing. To deny him his right to his own hurting, denies him the chance to the grappling you were allowed. Often the best one can do for another is to accompany him to his wounding *and leave him there.*

—⁓⁓

XXXIX

Getting closer

Am I free enough to pile these events as steps in my becoming?

Why must you wait until you *can* do it before you do it?

It is not what we've been through that matters, but where it has brought us that counts; not what we've suffered through, but the level from which we view it; not what others did to us but the fact that we lived through what they did; and that Christ walks with us beyond and upward, over and over and over.

There is a time to stand even though falling becomes inevitable.

A scar is significant of definite loss but not of continuous loss.

It is not the hurt that matters. It is the healing. To be healed you have to have been hurt. To be risen—to have fallen; to be reborn—to have gone through a dying.

Just knowing that He hears, He will act in the fullness of His time. Just reminding myself of these things lives my life out differently.

Perhaps it isn't the city in which you find yourself, the wisdom you've attained, the philosophy you embrace, as much as the fact that in turning your life, He may at last find you worthy to be instructed.

Maybe all of the waste is worth the arrival.

It is the thrust of agony that causes us to reach, to beg, to cry, to wait, to yield, to begin again—hushed, to listen. In the last analysis perhaps past scars are but ladders to be folded up when you have learned to live in the sudden burstingness of His presence, and in the long rivers of rapids that flow toward His thoughts.